This book belongs to:

....

If found, please return to:

....

UNPLUG EVERY DAY

365 Ways to Log Off and Live Better

CHRONICLE BOOKS

SAN FRANCISCO

ISBN: 978-1-4521-2895-5

Manufactured in China

MIX
Paper from
responsible sources
FSC
www.fsc.org   FSC® C104723

Designed by Jennifer Tolo Pierce
Illustrations by Danielle Kroll

10 9 8 7 6

Chronicle Books LLC
680 Second Street
San Francisco, California 94107
www.chroniclebooks.com

*This book could not have been created without
the thoughtful contributions of:*

Adair Lara, Alexandra Williams, Ali Presley, Alice Chau,
Amy Treadwell, Andrew LeValley, Caitlin Kirkpatrick,
Christina Mott, Emily Dubin, Genny McAuley, Guinevere
de la Mare, Heather Do, Jennifer Tolo Pierce, Joyce
Tomas, Kate Woodrow, Kelli Chipponeri, Laura Lee
Mattingly, Michelle Clair, Patricia Quan, Sarah Billingsley,
Sarah Higgins, Sarah Malarkey, and Shannon Sawtelle.

INTRODUCTION

Disconnect to reconnect!

We've all been guilty of the mid-dinner text message, the multitasked phone conversation, or the just-before-bedtime e-mail check. This journal offers you 365 small ways to detox from your technology. You'll find just enough prompts to help you appreciate your surroundings and be more at peace with your electronics.

Are you ready to start your digital detox? Flip through the pages of this journal and stop at any action that calls out to you the most today. These suggestions are meant to help you unplug from your digital companions and take your time, focus your attention, nurture your creativity, trust your memory, and enjoy your environment.

Have your ears been hidden by headphones for hours? Go to a live concert with a friend and enjoy the music together. Have you become reliant on your phone for directions? Pull out a paper map, leave the electronic version at home, and get lost on an adventure. Are you buried in e-mail? Spend an hour unsubscribing from lists that haunt you daily. Most of these actions are small enough to accomplish in a day, but they can have a big impact. They'll encourage you to take much-needed breaks and improve your habits to be more attentive. Use them as opportunities to turn off and tune in to the world around you.

When you have chosen a prompt, commit to completing it before the day is through and mark the page with a ribbon marker. Throughout the day, take moments to reflect on the effect the action has—on you, on your loved ones, or with complete strangers you may not have noticed if you'd been buried in your phone. At the end of the day, check off the prompt with the date of completion and jot down your observations on what you did. Have you found yourself less stressed? Are you more excited about taking adventures? Perhaps upon reflection, you'll want to enjoy the satisfaction of another digital detox tomorrow, the next day, and the day after.

WEAR A WATCH

instead of relying on your phone to tell time.

COMPLETED ON ....

REFLECT ....

....

....

ENJOY THE HERE AND NOW

instead of documenting for the there and later.

COMPLETED ON..

REFLECT...

....

....

DON'T
CHECK
E-MAIL

during your commute. Take the rare opportunity to
do absolutely nothing and let your mind wander.

COMPLETED ON ....

REFLECT ....

....

....

LAUGH OUT LOUD

instead of LOL. You might even make
someone else laugh, too.

COMPLETED ON...

REFLECT..

....

....

MAKE
A PHOTO
ALBUM

and relive each moment as you place
the photos on the page.

COMPLETED ON ....

REFLECT ....

....

....

START A JAR OF ACCOUNT- ABILITY

with your family. Anyone who checks a digital device during a live conversation has to put a quarter in the jar.

COMPLETED ON...

REFLECT...

....

....

POST
NEWS AND
NOTICES

on your school/work/community bulletin board.
You might be surprised by the responses.

COMPLETED ON ....

REFLECT ....

....

....

FOLLOW
A HIKING
TRAIL

instead of an e-mail trail, and enjoy
a spectacular view along the way.

COMPLETED ON...

REFLECT...

....

....

MEET AN ONLINE FRIEND IN PERSON.

COMPLETED ON ....

REFLECT ....

....

....

LEAVE YOUR PHONE AT HOME.

Plan in advance or leave things to chance.

COMPLETED ON...

REFLECT...

....

....

LISTEN UP!

Give someone your undivided attention.

COMPLETED ON ....

REFLECT ....

....

....

INSTALL A LANDLINE

and give your smartphone a break when at home.

COMPLETED ON..

REFLECT...

....

....

LIMIT
WEB SURFING

to one hour a day.

COMPLETED ON...

REFLECT...

....

....

SUPPORT YOUR LOCAL CRAFT FAIR.

COMPLETED ON...

REFLECT...

....

....

KEEP A
BIRTHDAY
BOOK

and never need an e-reminder again.

COMPLETED ON...

REFLECT...

....

....

START
A BOOK
CLUB.

COMPLETED ON..

REFLECT...

....

....

RUN
FOR FUN

and leave your mileage/elevation-gained
gadget at home.

COMPLETED ON ....

REFLECT ....

....

....

TAKE A BATH

and immerse yourself in a no-digital zone.

COMPLETED ON...

REFLECT...

....

....

ASK A STRANGER FOR DIRECTIONS

when you think you've lost your way.

COMPLETED ON ....

REFLECT ....

....

....

HAVE A PICNIC IN THE PARK

and enjoy your favorite spread rather
than a spreadsheet.

COMPLETED ON...

REFLECT..

....

....

LEARN
A NEW
LANGUAGE

that doesn't have "hyper" in its name.

COMPLETED ON ....

REFLECT ....

....

....

WRITE A LETTER TO THE EDITOR

instead of a blog post.

COMPLETED ON ....

REFLECT ....

....

....

SLOW DOWN.

COMPLETED ON ....

REFLECT ....

....

....

CHAT UP A STRANGER

when waiting in line.

COMPLETED ON ....

REFLECT ....

....

....

STUDY
THE
CLOUDS

and forecast the weather for yourself.

COMPLETED ON ....

REFLECT ....

....

....

HOST A NO-PHONES PARTY.

COMPLETED ON ....

REFLECT ....

....

....

Learn to

PLAY A
SONG ON
THE GUITAR.

COMPLETED ON...

REFLECT...

....

....

LISTEN

to a friend in need and experience
real peer-to-peer file sharing.

COMPLETED ON...

REFLECT...

....

....

SPEAK IN
PIG LATIN

with a friend to encrypt your public conversation.

REDUCE AMBIENT LIGHT

and digital hum. Turn off all digital devices
before going to bed.

COMPLETED ON ....

REFLECT ....

....

....

STUDY A SPIDERWEB

instead of the World Wide Web and appreciate
the genius of nature.

COMPLETED ON..

REFLECT...

....

....

INVITE SOMEONE FOR COFFEE.

COMPLETED ON...

REFLECT..

....

....

PRACTICE
A SONG
A CAPPELLA.

You'll impress your friends the next time
you're out on the town.

COMPLETED ON ....

REFLECT ....

....

....

LIMIT
DIGITAL
CLUTTER.

Designate a charging station.

COMPLETED ON..

REFLECT..

....

....

GO
ROLLER-
BLADING

or ice-skating and practice your inline
(rather than your online) skills.

COMPLETED ON ....

REFLECT ....

....

....

BROWSE A BOOKSTORE.

Take your time and explore.

COMPLETED ON...

REFLECT..

....

....

FINGER PAINT.

Enjoy the freedom of making a mess.

COMPLETED ON ....

REFLECT ....

....

....

OPEN THE WINDOWS

to refresh the air and your view.

COMPLETED ON..

REFLECT..

....

....

TRY AROMA- THERAPY

and reward your senses with a newfound calm (or energy).

COMPLETED ON ....

REFLECT ....

....

....

RUN AN OBSTACLE COURSE

to improve your own "mobile operating system."

COMPLETED ON...

REFLECT...

....

....

MAKE AN ORIGAMI PAPER CRANE

and share it with a young friend.

COMPLETED ON ....

REFLECT ....

....

....

ATTEND AN EVENT

and introduce yourself to three people
you've never met.

COMPLETED ON..

REFLECT...

....

....

REBOOT WITH BOOT CAMP

and feel the burn in a beneficial way.

COMPLETED ON

REFLECT

IMAGINE.

COMPLETED ON...

REFLECT...

....

....

IMPOSE A "NO PHONE" RULE

during meals out. The first person to check
for messages pays.

COMPLETED ON ....

REFLECT ....

....

....

PLAY
WITH
YOUR PET.

COMPLETED ON ....

REFLECT ....

....

....

WRITE
A SHORT
STORY

by hand.

COMPLETED ON ....

REFLECT ....

....

....

DOODLE DURING A MEETING.

Pen to paper will sharpen your focus (much more than checking e-mail).

COMPLETED ON..

REFLECT..

....

....

GET LOST.

Leave your map app behind and enjoy the adventure.

COMPLETED ON...

REFLECT..

....

....

GO
BOWLING

in a bowling alley instead of "bowling"
from your couch.

COMPLETED ON..

REFLECT..

....

....

WRITE YOUR GROCERY LIST

on a sheet of paper and keep it in your wallet.

COMPLETED ON..

REFLECT...

....

....

ROLL DOWN A GRASSY HILL.

Over and over again.

COMPLETED ON ....

REFLECT ....

....

....

GO FISHING ON A LAKE

and avoid being "phished" on the Internet.

COMPLETED ON ....

REFLECT ....

....

....

MAKE A PAPER SNOWFLAKE.

Then make another one.

COMPLETED ON...

REFLECT...

....

....

WALK
AROUND THE
BLOCK

for 15 minutes during your workday.

COMPLETED ON ....

REFLECT ....

....

....

COMB THROUGH YOUR STORAGE.

You might be surprised by the treasures you'll find.

COMPLETED ON..

REFLECT..

....

....

SUPPORT
LOCAL
BUSINESSES.

Treasures (and friendships) await in your own neighborhood.

COMPLETED ON ....

REFLECT ....

....

....

CHAT WITH A FRIEND,

not an avatar.

COMPLETED ON ....

REFLECT ....

....

....

GO
WITHOUT
SOCIAL
MEDIA

for a short time. Challenge yourself to go
for longer next time.

COMPLETED ON ....

REFLECT ....

....

....

UNPLUG CHARGERS

when not in use to save on your electrical bill
and give the planet a boost.

COMPLETED ON...

REFLECT..

....

....

START YOUR DAY WITH YOGA

to recharge your inner current.

COMPLETED ON ....

REFLECT ....

....

....

SWAP STORIES

with an elderly friend or family member.

COMPLETED ON...

REFLECT...

....

....

DONATE OLD ELECTRONICS

to a good cause.

COMPLETED ON ....

REFLECT ....

....

....

HOLD A YARD SALE

on a sunny day and unload without the upload.

COMPLETED ON...

REFLECT...

....

....

GO TO A FARM

and pick whatever is in season. Make a pie.

COMPLETED ON ....

REFLECT ....

....

....

ATTEND A TRIVIA GAME NIGHT,

and bolster your brain, no smartphones allowed.

COMPLETED ON...

REFLECT...

....

....

HANG AN INSPIRATION BOARD

by your desk. Creative solutions will be
only a glance away.

COMPLETED ON...

REFLECT...

....

....

HOST A CLOTHING SWAP

with friends and refresh your wardrobe without
a virtual shopping cart.

COMPLETED ON..

REFLECT...

....

....

GO FOR
A STROLL

and let nature (or the city) be your soundtrack.

COMPLETED ON...

REFLECT..

....

....

PRACTICE SINGLE-TASKING

and sharpen your focus by tackling
and completing one task at a time.

COMPLETED ON...

REFLECT...

....

....

CHECK
E-MAIL ONLY
EVERY TWO
HOURS

for a day.

COMPLETED ON

REFLECT

KEEP FRESH-CUT FLOWERS

in your home or office. Pause to breathe in the aromas while also giving your eyes a break from the screen.

COMPLETED ON...

REFLECT...

....

....

Make today

DIGITAL
DE-CLUTTER
DAY 1.

Gather up and e-cycle all outdated cords,
chargers, and devices.

COMPLETED ON ....

REFLECT ....

....

....

Make today

DIGITAL DE-CLUTTER DAY 2.

Take an hour or two to delete unnecessary e-mails
and lighten your digital load.

COMPLETED ON ....

REFLECT ....

....

....

BRUSH UP ON YOUR MATH SKILLS

by using your mental calculator
instead of a digital calculator.

COMPLETED ON ....

REFLECT ....

....

....

VISIT A PUBLIC GARDEN.

Stop and smell the roses.

COMPLETED ON ....

REFLECT ....

....

....

LIST THE PLACES YOU'VE TRAVELED.

Then make a list of places you'd still like to visit.

COMPLETED ON ....

REFLECT ....

....

....

HOLD
SOMEONE'S
HAND

and experience the true meaning of "handheld."

COMPLETED ON..

REFLECT..

....

....

FIGHT
THE
C-SLUMP.

Do a posture check every 10 minutes
you're at the computer.

COMPLETED ON...

REFLECT...

....

....

BUILD
A FORT

with a young friend using the boxes from online
deliveries. Then take a pledge to shop local.

COMPLETED ON ....

REFLECT ....

....

....

Learn to

RECITE A POEM FROM MEMORY.

COMPLETED ON ....

REFLECT ....

....

....

CELEBRATE

National Day of Unplugging.

COMPLETED ON..

REFLECT..

....

....

INSTITUTE
A NO-TECH
TUESDAY

and turn off all digital devices for at least three hours.

COMPLETED ON ....

REFLECT ....

....

....

SUPPORT YOUR LOCAL POST OFFICE

and flood a friend's "inbox" with surprise notes and gifts.

COMPLETED ON ....

REFLECT ....

....

....

READ A BOOK TO A CHILD,

and send the best kind of instant message.

COMPLETED ON ....

REFLECT ....

....

....

Close your eyes and

TAKE
FIVE DEEP
BREATHS.

COMPLETED ON...

REFLECT...

....

....

HOST A COSTUME PARTY

and bring your inner avatar to life.

COMPLETED ON...

REFLECT...

....

....

GO ON A NONVIRTUAL DATE.

COMPLETED ON...

REFLECT...

....

....

EAT LUNCH

away from your computer.

COMPLETED ON ....

REFLECT ....

....

....

CONSIDER

how many times a day you reference what
a friend said through social media.

COMPLETED ON..

REFLECT...

....

....

KEEP A GREEN PLANT

at your desk and enjoy the benefits of
cellulose over silicon.

COMPLETED ON ....

REFLECT ....

....

....

PRACTICE PATIENCE

while waiting in line and resist the distraction
of a smartphone.

COMPLETED ON...

REFLECT...

....

....

DON'T
WALK AND
TEXT.

COMPLETED ON ....

REFLECT ....

....

....

TAKE A SURFING CLASS.

Learn how to surf the waves instead of the Web.

COMPLETED ON..

REFLECT..

....

....

ATTEND A REUNION

and "find friends" face-to-face.

COMPLETED ON ....

REFLECT ....

....

....

SAY GOOD MORNING

to at least three strangers.

COMPLETED ON..

REFLECT...

....

....

VISIT
A NEW
NEIGHBOR-
HOOD

and browse the local stores.

COMPLETED ON ....

REFLECT ....

....

....

WATCH A MOVIE AT THE DRIVE-IN,

the ultimate antidote to watching movies on a laptop.

COMPLETED ON ....

REFLECT ....

....

....

SAY YES.

COMPLETED ON...

REFLECT..

....

....

BAKE
COOKIES

and share.

COMPLETED ON ....

REFLECT ....

....

....

COMMIT
TO
UNPLUGGING

for a short time every day for a week.

COMPLETED ON..

REFLECT..

....

....

PET A CAT
OR A DOG

and give the mouse a rest.

COMPLETED ON..

REFLECT..

....

....

VOLUNTEER FOR A CAUSE

in person instead of simply signing an e-petition.

COMPLETED ON ....

REFLECT ....

....

....

USE A WALL CALENDAR

to keep track of engagements.

COMPLETED ON..

REFLECT...

....

....

SUBSCRIBE TO A PRINT MAGAZINE.

COMPLETED ON...

REFLECT...

....

....

PASS
A NOTE

and reexperience the thrill of covert
communication, junior high–style.

COMPLETED ON...

REFLECT...

....

....

FILL A
BINDER

with your favorite recipes.

COMPLETED ON ....

REFLECT ....

....

....

GIVE SOMEONE A SMILE

instead of a :).

COMPLETED ON ....

REFLECT ....

....

....

WATCH THE SUN SET.

Your camera app filter will never be as good.

COMPLETED ON..

REFLECT...

....

....

TAKE THE LONG WAY.

COMPLETED ON...

REFLECT..

....

....

CHOOSE
PEOPLE

over pixels.

TAKE A
WALKING
TOUR

of your town.

COMPLETED ON..

REFLECT..

....

....

PRACTICE
CORRECT
SPELLING

without autocorrect.

COMPLETED ON ....

REFLECT ....

....

....

SEND A THANK-YOU NOTE.

COMPLETED ON ....

REFLECT ....

....

....

DRAW A
PICTURE.

COMPLETED ON ....

REFLECT ....

....

....

RAKE A PATCH OF LEAVES.

Play in them as you did when you were younger.

COMPLETED ON...

REFLECT...

....

....

EXERCISE WITHOUT HEADPHONES.

Listen to the sound of your breathing.

COMPLETED ON ....

REFLECT ....

....

....

FIND A
PHOTO
BOOTH.

COMPLETED ON ....

REFLECT ....

....

....

START A LOOKBOOK

of your favorite fashion finds, using magazines,
catalogs, and other tactile materials.

COMPLETED ON

REFLECT

IGNORE STATUS UPDATES.

Call a friend to really find out what's going on in his life.

COMPLETED ON...

REFLECT...

....

....

PLAY HOOKY.

COMPLETED ON ....

REFLECT ....

....

....

FIND A BODY OF WATER.

Close your eyes and enjoy the sounds.

COMPLETED ON..

REFLECT..

....

....

UNSUB-
SCRIBE

from excess e-mails.

COMPLETED ON ....

REFLECT ....

....

....

OPEN A
DICTIONARY.

Discover at least five new words as you
flip through the pages.

COMPLETED ON...

REFLECT...

....

....

USE A GUIDEBOOK

to plan your next trip.

COMPLETED ON ....

REFLECT ....

....

....

STARGAZE.

CLIP COUPONS

to save on local deals.

COMPLETED ON..

REFLECT...

....

....

COMPLI-
MENT
SOMEONE.

It means more than virtual approval.

COMPLETED ON ....

REFLECT ....

....

....

TAG YOUR FRIENDS

in an impromptu game of freeze tag.

COMPLETED ON ....

REFLECT ....

....

....

GO OUT
FOR
KARAOKE

and bring your dream playlist to life.

COMPLETED ON ....

REFLECT ....

....

....

WAIT
10 MINUTES

before responding to e-mails or text messages.

COMPLETED ON...

REFLECT...

....

....

VISIT
AN ART
MUSEUM.

COMPLETED ON..

REFLECT..

....

....

BALANCE YOUR CHECKBOOK.

COMPLETED ON ....

REFLECT ....

....

....

CHANGE
THE SHEETS

on your bed.

COMPLETED ON ....

REFLECT ....

....

....

READ
A COMIC
BOOK.

COMPLETED ON...

REFLECT..

....

....

LOG OFF
A SOCIAL
NETWORK

for a week. Could you do without it for longer?

COMPLETED ON ....

REFLECT ....

....

....

COMPLI-MENT THE CHEF

or waiter at a restaurant, instead of writing an online review later.

COMPLETED ON...

REFLECT...

....

....

COOK
SOMETHING

you know how to make from memory.

COMPLETED ON...

REFLECT..

....

....

DECLARE AN ANCESTOR'S DAY,

during which you can't do anything a grandparent couldn't.

COMPLETED ON ....

REFLECT ....

....

....

PRINT AND FRAME PICTURES.

COMPLETED ON ....

REFLECT ....

....

....

DRIVE

with the windows down and the radio off.

COMPLETED ON ....

REFLECT ....

....

....

GO FLY A KITE.

COMPLETED ON ....

REFLECT ....

....

....

DRINK
WATER.

Take a break from your screen and hydrate every few hours.

COMPLETED ON ....

REFLECT ....

....

....

WRITE
A LETTER

every day for a week.

COMPLETED ON..

REFLECT...

....

....

FIND A CAFÉ WITH NO WI-FI,

and actually talk to the person next to you about the coffee.

COMPLETED ON ....

REFLECT ....

....

....

TRY DATING
OLD-SCHOOL

and meet someone new at the market/at a bar
rather than looking at online profiles.

COMPLETED ON ....

REFLECT ....

....

....

GO FOR A RUN/HIKE/ WALK

and don't map it.

COMPLETED ON ....

REFLECT ....

....

....

GO TO A
MUSEUM

and sketch your favorite painting in a notebook.

COMPLETED ON ....

REFLECT ....

....

....

Download an app to

CUT OFF YOUR INTERNET

access for one hour every day. See how much you get done.

COMPLETED ON ....

REFLECT ....

....

....

GO TO A RECORD STORE

and buy something. Admire the album art.

COMPLETED ON ....

REFLECT ....

....

....

GO TO
A CAFÉ

with just a book in hand.

COMPLETED ON ....

REFLECT ....

....

....

HAVE A QUESTION?

Ask a newspaper advice columnist,
not an online chat forum.

COMPLETED ON ....

REFLECT ....

....

....

INSPIRE SOMEONE ELSE.

Post a message on all social media channels
that you're taking the day to unplug.

COMPLETED ON ....

REFLECT ....

....

....

REALLY
CHECK IN

instead of "checking in".

COMPLETED ON ....

REFLECT ....

....

....

REMOVE
E-MAIL
CAPABILITY

from your phone. Try it for a week and
see if you want to keep going.

COMPLETED ON ....

REFLECT ....

....

....

START A
JOURNAL

and commit to writing just one line a day.

COMPLETED ON...

REFLECT...

....

....

PLAY A GAME OF I SPY

with some young friends.

COMPLETED ON ....

REFLECT ....

....

....

JOIN
A CLUB.

COMPLETED ON ....

REFLECT ....

....

....

TAKE A SAILING LESSON.

COMPLETED ON...

REFLECT...

....

....

KEEP THE TELEVISION OFF

all evening.

COMPLETED ON..

REFLECT..

....

....

LOAN A FAVORITE BOOK

to a friend.

COMPLETED ON ....

REFLECT ....

....

....

GO TO A LECTURE

on a topic you know nothing about.

COMPLETED ON ....

REFLECT ....

....

....

MAKE A "TV"

out of a cardboard box with your favorite young friend.
Put on your own reality show.

COMPLETED ON ....

REFLECT ....

....

....

MAKE A
POINT

to not have a screen be the first and
last thing you see today.

COMPLETED ON...

REFLECT...

....

....

MEDITATE.

COMPLETED ON ....

REFLECT ....

....

....

MAKE SOMETHING

with your hands. Allow yourself to learn and fail,
and don't seek the answers on the Internet.

COMPLETED ON ....

REFLECT ....

....

....

DON'T RETRACE YOUR STEPS.

Take a different route instead.

COMPLETED ON ....

REFLECT ....

....

....

GO
FISHING.

COMPLETED ON ....

REFLECT ....

....

....

TRY
A NEW
FRUIT.

COMPLETED ON..

REFLECT...

....

....

ORGANIZE
YOUR
ROOM

instead of your computer desktop.

COMPLETED ON ....

REFLECT ....

....

....

PEOPLE
WATCH

at an interesting street corner.

COMPLETED ON ....

REFLECT ....

....

....

PLAN A CANDLELIT NIGHT

—no electricity or electronics allowed.

COMPLETED ON..

REFLECT...

....

....

SEND PAPER INVITES

to your next party.

COMPLETED ON..

REFLECT..

....

....

PLAY A DRAWING GAME.

Start a drawing, fold the paper, and pass to someone else to finish.

COMPLETED ON ....

REFLECT ....

....

....

PLAY OUTSIDE.

COMPLETED ON ....

REFLECT ....

....

....

DO THE DISHES BY HAND

for a day.

COMPLETED ON..

REFLECT..

....

....

SWEAR OFF ONLINE GAMES

for a week.

COMPLETED ON ....

REFLECT ....

....

....

CALL A
FRIEND,

just because.

COMPLETED ON ....

REFLECT ....

....

....

MAKE A
FRIENDSHIP
BRACELET.

COMPLETED ON..

REFLECT..

....

....

REMEMBER SKIPPING?

Try it.

COMPLETED ON...

REFLECT...

....

....

TREAT
YOURSELF

to a beautiful fountain pen.

COMPLETED ON ....

REFLECT ....

....

....

EXPLORE.

COMPLETED ON..

REFLECT..

....

....

SHOW UP

at a friend's house unannounced.

COMPLETED ON ....

REFLECT ....

....

....

SMILE
AT A
STRANGER.

COMPLETED ON..

REFLECT...

....

....

MEET YOUR NEIGHBOR.

COMPLETED ON ....

REFLECT ....

....

....

TAKE A CALLIGRAPHY CLASS

and practice the art of letter writing.

COMPLETED ON ....

REFLECT ....

....

....

PLANT
SOMETHING.

COMPLETED ON ....

REFLECT ....

....

....

TAKE A NEW ROUTE.

COMPLETED ON..

REFLECT...

....

....

LEAVE YOUR PHONE AT HOME.

COMPLETED ON...

REFLECT...

....

....

TAKE A TECHNOLOGY SABBATH

on the weekend. Don't use any electricity
from sundown to sundown.

COMPLETED ON ....

REFLECT ....

....

....

BAKE
A CAKE

for an elderly neighbor.

COMPLETED ON ....

REFLECT ....

....

....

THROW
A DART

at the map of your town and
have a picnic where it lands.

COMPLETED ON ....

REFLECT ....

....

....

USE A TYPEWRITER

or write your notes by hand.

COMPLETED ON ....

REFLECT ....

....

....

VISIT A FRIEND

at his workplace rather than sending an e-mail.

COMPLETED ON..

REFLECT..

....

....

PLAY
DODGEBALL.

COMPLETED ON..

REFLECT..

....

....

DON'T SET
AN ALARM
CLOCK

—instead, wake up with the sun.

COMPLETED ON..

REFLECT...

....

....

LEARN
THE
HARMONICA.

COMPLETED ON ....

REFLECT ....

....

....

BRAINSTORM WITH A FRIEND

when you can't remember the name of a movie
(or book or song), instead of looking it up online.

COMPLETED ON...

REFLECT...

....

....

VISIT
THE
LIBRARY.

COMPLETED ON ....

REFLECT ....

....

....

DRIVE

without taking a call.

COMPLETED ON ....

REFLECT ....

....

....

PLAY
WITH A
YOUNG ONE

using physical toys instead of gadgets.

COMPLETED ON

REFLECT

ASK
YOUR
WAITER

when you're not sure of an ingredient on a menu.

COMPLETED ON ....

REFLECT ....

....

....

HANG
OUT

with someone and reconnect.

COMPLETED ON ....

REFLECT ....

....

....

ENCOURAGE
A FRIEND

to digital-detox for a day.

COMPLETED ON ....

REFLECT ....

....

....

LOG YOUR TECH USAGE.

What surprised you?

COMPLETED ON ....

REFLECT ....

....

....

DISCOVER
A NEW
RESTAURANT

in the food section of your local newspaper
and make a reservation.

COMPLETED ON ....

REFLECT ....

....

....

PUT YOUR PHONE ON SILENT

and check it only once an hour.

COMPLETED ON ....

REFLECT ....

....

....

CALL SOME-
ONE OUT OF
THE BLUE.

COMPLETED ON..

REFLECT...

....

....

DROP A
QUARTER

in an old-school arcade game machine.

COMPLETED ON..

REFLECT...

....

....

GET A LIBRARY CARD

and check out the maximum number of books.

COMPLETED ON ....

REFLECT ....

....

....

COMMU-NICATE IN PERSON

for a day. Leave your text messages off and vow not to send e-mails.

COMPLETED ON..

REFLECT..

....

....

REVISIT A FAVORITE COOKBOOK

for new recipe ideas.

COMPLETED ON ....

REFLECT ....

....

....

WAKE UP, SHOWER, AND EAT

before checking e-mail.

COMPLETED ON ....

REFLECT ....

....

....

BUY A DISPOSABLE CAMERA.

Revel in the anticipation of waiting for
your photos to be developed.

COMPLETED ON ....

REFLECT...

....

....

GO BIRD-WATCHING.

COMPLETED ON ....

REFLECT ....

....

....

SURPRISE
SOMEONE.

COMPLETED ON ....

REFLECT ....

....

....

GO TO
A FLEA
MARKET

and explore.

COMPLETED ON ....

REFLECT ....

....

....

HAVE
CONFIDENCE

in your memory, and experience
an event without taking photos.

COMPLETED ON ....

REFLECT...

....

....

START A CAMPFIRE.

COMPLETED ON..

REFLECT..

....

....

RIDE
YOUR BIKE.

COMPLETED ON

REFLECT

CHAT UP
THE STAFF

at you local grocer for new ideas on how to cook
a vegetable or fruit.

COMPLETED ON..

REFLECT..

....

....

WALK
TO A
PLACE

you normally reach by car or public transit.

COMPLETED ON ....

REFLECT ....

....

....

TRY OUT A
RESTAURANT

without checking online reviews.

COMPLETED ON ....

REFLECT ....

....

....

VISIT A NATIONAL PARK.

COMPLETED ON ....

REFLECT ....

....

....

PLAY A BOARD GAME

if you ever find yourself bored.

COMPLETED ON ....

REFLECT ....

....

....

DON'T
UPDATE

any social media for two days. How did it make you feel?

COMPLETED ON...

REFLECT...

....

....

SLOWLY
CHEW
YOUR FOOD

instead of photographing it.

COMPLETED ON ....

REFLECT ....

....

....

PLAN
A SPA
DAY.

COMPLETED ON ....

REFLECT ....

....

....

GO TO A FARMERS' MARKET.

Talk to a farmer about the produce.

COMPLETED ON ....

REFLECT ....

....

....

TAKE A
BREAK

and drop by a co-worker's desk.

COMPLETED ON ....

REFLECT ....

....

....

PLAN
A TRIP

with a travel agent.

COMPLETED ON ....

REFLECT ....

....

....

SEND A CARE PACKAGE

to someone who needs it.

COMPLETED ON ....

REFLECT ....

....

....

BUY A NEWSPAPER.

Read it from cover to cover.

COMPLETED ON ....

REFLECT ....

....

....

GO ON
A HIKE

and look as far ahead into the distance as the eye can see.

COMPLETED ON ....

REFLECT ....

....

....

BECOME
A
PEN PAL

with a distant friend. Commit to writing two letters a month.

COMPLETED ON ....

REFLECT ....

....

....

LOOK UP, NOT DOWN.

COMPLETED ON..

REFLECT..

....

....

REDUCE YOUR E-MAILS BY HALF

by conversing in person.

COMPLETED ON ....

REFLECT ....

....

....

HAVE A FAMILY GAME NIGHT.

COMPLETED ON ....

REFLECT ....

....

....

BUY A NEW BICYCLE.

COMPLETED ON ....

REFLECT ....

....

....

GO OFF THE GRID.

Reconnect with nature in a "no service" zone.

COMPLETED ON..

REFLECT..

....

....

MAKE A TO-DO LIST

using pen and paper. Relish the satisfaction
of crossing things off by hand.

COMPLETED ON ....

REFLECT ....

....

....

TAKE A DIGITAL-FREE VACATION

and recharge yourself instead of your devices.

COMPLETED ON..

REFLECT...

....

....

WATCH
A PLAY

or musical instead of a movie.

COMPLETED ON..

REFLECT...

....

....

GO THROUGH PHOTOS.

Relish a pre-digital era.

COMPLETED ON ....

REFLECT ....

....

....

PLAY WITH CUTE DOGS/CATS/ BABIES,

instead of taking photos of them.

COMPLETED ON ....

REFLECT ....

....

....

GO TO A CONCERT.

COMPLETED ON..

REFLECT..

....

....

STRETCH
YOUR
LEGS.

COMPLETED ON ....

REFLECT ....

....

....

RESIST
THE URGE

to look at a screen while in conversation.

COMPLETED ON ....

REFLECT ....

....

....

WALK TO THE VIDEO STORE

and rent a movie instead of streaming online videos.

COMPLETED ON ....

REFLECT ....

....

....

CARRY A JOURNAL

and jot down observations throughout the day.

COMPLETED ON...

REFLECT...

....

....

LIMIT DIGITAL SNACKING

to certain hours a day. It will make for a
healthier waistline and a more restful mind.

COMPLETED ON..

REFLECT...

....

....

COOK
WITHOUT
A CLOCK.

Use your intuition.

COMPLETED ON..

REFLECT..

....

....

SKIP
THE GYM

and exercise outdoors.

COMPLETED ON ....

REFLECT ....

....

....

RELAX ON THE COUCH

without turning on or plugging in.

COMPLETED ON...

REFLECT...

....

....

USE
ARITHMETIC

to calculate the dinner tip on the back
of your receipt.

COMPLETED ON...

REFLECT...

....

....

SPEND TIME OUTDOORS.

COMPLETED ON...

REFLECT..

....

....

DON'T
CHECK YOUR
PHONE

unless it rings.

COMPLETED ON ....

REFLECT ....

....

....

DUST OFF YOUR RECORD PLAYER

and bring out your vinyls.

COMPLETED ON..

REFLECT...

....

....

HOP ON
THE BUS

with no destination in mind. Get off
on a whim and wander.

COMPLETED ON...

REFLECT..

....

....

ORGANIZE YOUR CLOSET.

COMPLETED ON...

REFLECT...

....

....

DON'T PLUG IN

for your entire commute.

COMPLETED ON...

REFLECT..

....

....

SET UP A LEMONADE STAND

to raise money instead of online crowd funding.

COMPLETED ON..

REFLECT...

....

....

READ THE FLYERS

on your local bulletin board to discover new things.

COMPLETED ON...

REFLECT...

....

....

GIVE A PRE-SENTATION

without using software or a projector.

COMPLETED ON ....

REFLECT ....

....

....

FALL ASLEEP
WITH
A BOOK.

COMPLETED ON..

REFLECT..

....

....

PICK UP
TRASH

around your block instead of deleting virtual trash.

COMPLETED ON ....

REFLECT ....

....

....

CHOOSE THE CASHIER

over self-checkout.

COMPLETED ON ....

REFLECT ....

....

....

SKIP THE VENDING MACHINE

and cook yourself a healthful snack.

COMPLETED ON..

REFLECT...

....

....

PAY ATTENTION.

COMPLETED ON ....

REFLECT ....

....

....

TAKE A DEEP BREATH

and smile. Repeat.

COMPLETED ON ....

REFLECT ....

....

....

EXERCISE

without looking at a clock.

COMPLETED ON...

REFLECT...

....

....

SMILE

when you talk on the phone.

COMPLETED ON ....

REFLECT ....

....

....

TAKE
A CLASS.

COMPLETED ON ....

REFLECT ....

....

....

SHARE
YOUR
THOUGHTS

with the person nearest to you,
not people on the Internet.

COMPLETED ON..

REFLECT..

....

....

FIND
A SLIDE

and slide down it.

COMPLETED ON ....

REFLECT ....

....

....

CLOSE
YOUR EYES

during your next meal.

COMPLETED ON..

REFLECT..

....

....

INSIST
ON
HELPING

your busiest friend with one thing
he needs to get done.

COMPLETED ON ....

REFLECT ....

....

....

CLEAN OUT YOUR JUNK DRAWER

and relish clearing out physical clutter.

COMPLETED ON

REFLECT

PUT CASH
IN A PIGGY
BANK

instead of depositing it.

COMPLETED ON ....

REFLECT ....

....

....

MAKE EYE CONTACT.

COMPLETED ON ....

REFLECT ....

....

....

ASK
SOMEONE
TO DANCE.

COMPLETED ON ....

REFLECT ....

....

....

CONDUCT RESEARCH AT A LIBRARY.

COMPLETED ON ....

REFLECT ....

....

....

CREATE
A DIY
PROJECT

using just your imagination.

COMPLETED ON ....

REFLECT ....

....

....

LET YOUR PHONE DIE.

COMPLETED ON..

REFLECT..

....

....

AVOID THE MICRO-WAVE

when preparing all your meals for the day.

COMPLETED ON ....

REFLECT ....

....

....

LOCATE THE SOURCE OF WHITE NOISE

and see if you can eradicate it.

COMPLETED ON..

REFLECT..

....

....

TAKE
A POWER
NAP

to reboot.

COMPLETED ON ....

REFLECT ....

....

....

LINE—DRY YOUR LAUNDRY.

COMPLETED ON..

REFLECT..

....

....

INVENT
A NEW
RECIPE.

COMPLETED ON ....

REFLECT ....

....

....

GO TO A MUSEUM

to find inspiration instead of clicking
through a slideshow.

COMPLETED ON ....

REFLECT ....

....

....

LISTEN
TO A RADIO
PROGRAM.

COMPLETED ON...

REFLECT...

....

....

LEAVE YOUR FAVORITE BOOK

in a public place with a note to a stranger.

COMPLETED ON ....

REFLECT ....

....

....

LISTEN TO YOUR PARTNER

about her day.

COMPLETED ON ....

REFLECT ....

....

....

DECOM-PRESS

by doing anything that doesn't require pressing buttons.

COMPLETED ON ....

REFLECT ....

....

....

START
UP
A BOOK,

not a computer.

COMPLETED ON ....

REFLECT ....

....

....

POST YOUR THOUGHTS

to a shared refrigerator, and not a forum.

TAKE
THE
STAIRS.

COMPLETED ON ....

REFLECT ....

....

....

LEAVE CHALK MESSAGES

on the sidewalk.

COMPLETED ON ....

REFLECT ....

....

....

EAT SOMETHING NEW.

Learn through experience, not research.

COMPLETED ON ....

REFLECT ....

....

....

GO ON AN ADVENTURE.

COMPLETED ON...

REFLECT...

....

....

HAVE A BLOCK PARTY

and get to know your neighbors.

COMPLETED ON ....

REFLECT ....

....

....

DETOX

from a different digital medium each day of the week.

COMPLETED ON ....

REFLECT ....

....

....

DO
WHATEVER
ELSE

you would be doing if you weren't digitally immersed.

COMPLETED ON ....

REFLECT ....

....

....

DISCONNECT

your home Internet for a weekend.

COMPLETED ON..

REFLECT..

....

....

MEMORIZE THE PHONE NUMBER

of someone you call often but usually speed dial.

COMPLETED ON ....

REFLECT ....

....

....

WRITE DOWN A LIST

of things you're grateful for and tape it to your wall.

COMPLETED ON ....

REFLECT ....

....

....

SEND A MESSAGE IN A BOTTLE.

COMPLETED ON..

REFLECT..

....

....

LISTEN TO
AN ALBUM

from start to finish instead of listening
to your playlist on shuffle.

COMPLETED ON..

REFLECT...

....

....

PITCH
A TENT

in your backyard and sleep under the sky.

COMPLETED ON ....

REFLECT ....

....

....

ATTEND AN A CAPPELLA SHOW.

COMPLETED ON ....

REFLECT ....

....

....

LEAVE
WORK
BEHIND

once you leave the office.

COMPLETED ON ....

REFLECT ....

....

....

Gather some friends and

CREATE A MASSAGE TRAIN.

COMPLETED ON ....

REFLECT ....

....

....

TAKE A
5-MINUTE
BREAK

outside.

COMPLETED ON ....

REFLECT ....

....

....

SKETCH YOUR SUR-ROUNDINGS

while waiting in line.

COMPLETED ON ....

REFLECT ....

....

....

PICK
A COLOR

and try to notice everything around
you in that color.

COMPLETED ON..

REFLECT...

....

....

ASSUME
A YOGA
POSE

and keep it for a minute. Then try another.

COMPLETED ON..

REFLECT...

....

....

ASK A STRANGER

for his favorite to-do recommendations.

COMPLETED ON ....

REFLECT ....

....

....

HAVE AN IN-PERSON CONVERSA- TION

for every e-mail you send.

COMPLETED ON...

REFLECT..

....

....

USE A
LAVENDER
EYE PILLOW

to relax your eye muscles before you go to sleep.

COMPLETED ON ....

REFLECT ....

....

....

GO ON
A DAY
ADVENTURE,

map it down on paper, and share it with a friend.

COMPLETED ON ....

REFLECT...

....

....

WRITE
A NOTE

to a stranger. Put it in a random mailbox.

COMPLETED ON..

REFLECT...

....

....

USE THE SUN AND SHADOWS TO TELL TIME.

COMPLETED ON ....

REFLECT ....

....

....

KICK OFF
YOUR
SHOES,

sit back, and relax.

COMPLETED ON ....

REFLECT ....

....

....

PLAY A WRITING GAME.

Start a sentence, fold the paper, and pass to another person to continue the story.

COMPLETED ON

REFLECT

SEND
FLOWERS

instead of a text message.

COMPLETED ON ....

REFLECT ....

....

....

CROSS OFF AN ITEM

on your bucket list.

COMPLETED ON ....

REFLECT ....

....

....

LEAVE
A NOTE

in your partner's lunch sack.

COMPLETED ON...

REFLECT...

....

....

DO A
CROSSWORD
PUZZLE

on your commute.

COMPLETED ON...

REFLECT...

....

....

REREAD YOUR FAVORITE BOOK.

COMPLETED ON ....

REFLECT ....

....

....

PULL WEEDS

from the cracks of the sidewalk in front
of your house.

COMPLETED ON ....

REFLECT ....

....

....

STRETCH

for 10 minutes before you go to bed.

COMPLETED ON...

REFLECT..

....

....

CUT OUT BACKGROUND MUSIC

for a day. Do you appreciate music even more after?

COMPLETED ON..

REFLECT..

....

....

GO
BAREFOOT.

COMPLETED ON ....

REFLECT ....

....

....

TRY TO
FIX
SOMETHING

that's broken instead of buying a new one.

COMPLETED ON..

REFLECT..

....

....

TRY A NEW DISH

at your favorite restaurant.

COMPLETED ON ....

REFLECT ....

....

....

PLAY
DOMINOS.

COMPLETED ON ....

REFLECT ....

....

....

LOOK UP AT THE SKY

and try to find animals in the clouds
as you did when you were a kid.

COMPLETED ON ....

REFLECT ....

....

....

BUY THE ALBUM

directly from the merchandise table at a concert
instead of downloading it later.

COMPLETED ON...

REFLECT...

....

....

GO TO A BANK TELLER,

not a machine, when you need to withdraw money.

COMPLETED ON...

REFLECT..

....

....

LEARN
TO KNIT.

COMPLETED ON...

REFLECT...

....

....

START
A HAIKU
JOURNAL.

COMPLETED ON

REFLECT

JUMP
ROPE.

COMPLETED ON ....

REFLECT ....

....

....

SHARE
FAVORITE
BOOKS

with a friend.

COMPLETED ON

REFLECT

WRITE
A NEWSY
LETTER

to a relative.

COMPLETED ON...

REFLECT...

....

....

SELECT A THANK-YOU CARD

after attending a party and write an appreciative note
to the hostess.

COMPLETED ON

REFLECT

ASK A PASSERBY

for his favorite local spots to explore.

COMPLETED ON...

REFLECT...

....

....

HEAD
TO THE
BEACH

for the day.

COMPLETED ON ....

REFLECT ....

....

....

GRAB A
SEWING
KIT

and mend those needy items of clothing.

COMPLETED ON ....

REFLECT ....

....

....

WRITE YOUR MEMOIR

on your favorite paper.

COMPLETED ON..

REFLECT...

....

....

TAKE
A WALK

and see if you can name the trees
in your neighborhood.

COMPLETED ON...

REFLECT..

....

....

GO BERRY PICKING.

COMPLETED ON ....

REFLECT ....

....

....

MAKE
A CARD

for a friend.

COMPLETED ON ....

REFLECT ....

....

....

GROW
SOME
HERBS

on your kitchen windowsill.

COMPLETED ON..

REFLECT...

....

....

TAKE A HIKE

and see how many wild plants you can name.

COMPLETED ON ....

REFLECT ....

....

....

RIDE
YOUR BIKE

on a new route.

COMPLETED ON ....

REFLECT ....

....

....

GET A MASSAGE.

COMPLETED ON

REFLECT

EAT YOUR LUNCH ALONE

and in silence.

COMPLETED ON..

REFLECT..

....

....

LEARN
A NEW
SPORT.

COMPLETED ON..

REFLECT..

....

....

BRING
FLOWERS

to someone you know who seldom gets out.

COMPLETED ON

REFLECT

TRY A NEW COFFEE DRINK.

COMPLETED ON ....

REFLECT ....

....

....

SORT YOUR COINS

into paper tubes and take them to the bank.

COMPLETED ON ....

REFLECT ....

....

....

TAKE A DANCE LESSON.

COMPLETED ON ....

REFLECT ....

....

....

PLAY
SOLITAIRE

with a deck of real cards.

COMPLETED ON ....

REFLECT ....

....

....

GO HORSEBACK RIDING.

COMPLETED ON ....

REFLECT ....

....

....

CLEAN OUT THE REFRIG- ERATOR.

COMPLETED ON ....

REFLECT ....

....

....

What else can you do?

COMPLETED ON ....

REFLECT ....

....

....

What else can you do?

What else can you do?

COMPLETED ON ....

REFLECT ....

....

....

What else can you do?

COMPLETED ON ....

REFLECT ....

....

....

What else can you do?

COMPLETED ON

REFLECT

What else can you do?

COMPLETED ON ....

REFLECT ....

....

....

What else can you do?

COMPLETED ON ....

REFLECT ....

....

....

Chronicle Books publishes distinctive books and gifts. From award-winning children's titles, bestselling cookbooks, and eclectic pop culture to acclaimed works of art and design, stationery, and journals, we craft publishing that's instantly recognizable for its spirit and creativity. Enjoy our publishing and become part of our community at www.chroniclebooks.com.